Cell Wars

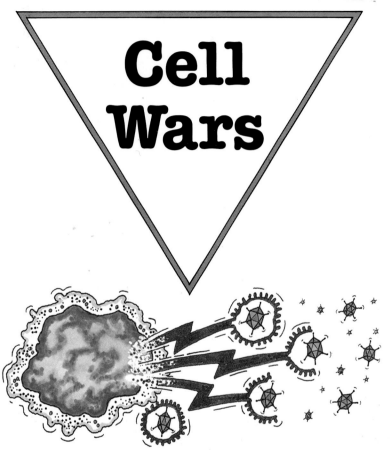

by Dr. Fran Balkwill
illustrated by Mic Rolph

Carolrhoda Books, Inc./Minneapolis

This edition first published 1993 by Carolrhoda Books, Inc.

Library of Congress Cataloging-in-Publication Data

Balkwill, Frances R.
    Cell wars / by Fran Balkwill ; illustrated by Mic Rolph.
        p.   cm.
    Originally published: London : W. Collins, 1990.
    Summary: Explains how cells fight off diseases and viruses
in the human body.
    ISBN 0-87614-761-9
    1. Cellular immunity – Juvenile literature. [1. Immune
system.] I. Rolph, Mic, ill. II. Title.
QR185.5.B36   1993
616.07'9 – dc20   92-6377
                                                      CIP
                                                       AC

Manufactured in the United States of America

1   2   3   4   5   6   7   8   9   10   02   01   00   99   98   97   96   95   94   93

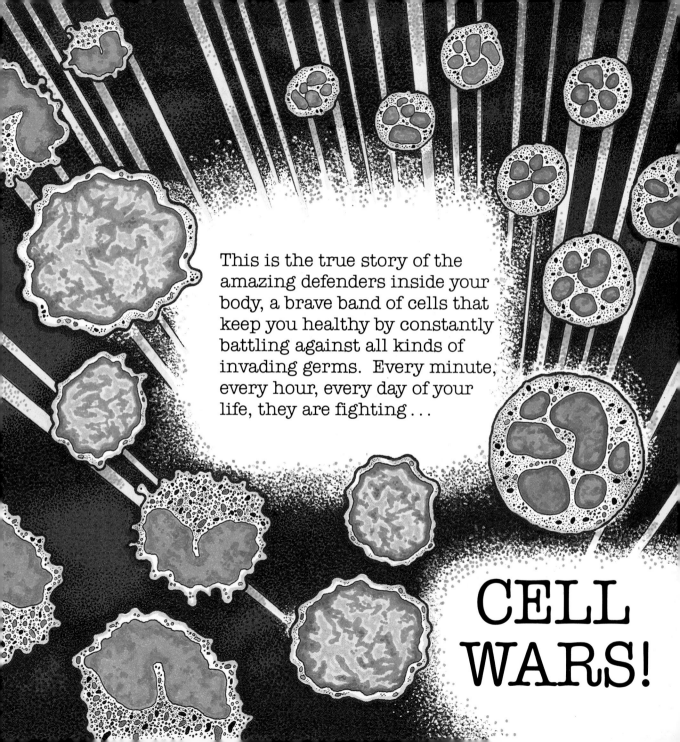

This is the true story of the amazing defenders inside your body, a brave band of cells that keep you healthy by constantly battling against all kinds of invading germs. Every minute, every hour, every day of your life, they are fighting...

CELL WARS!

Every part of your body is made of tiny building blocks called **cells** — more than ten million million of them! The muscles that make you move are made from cells. The nerves that make you see, feel, hear, smell, and taste things are made of cells. The bones that hold your body up are made from cells. Cells make your hair and your teeth, your nose and your eyes. Skin cells are very clever. They form a tough layer of dead cells all over your body that protects you from bumps, thumps, and germs.

But sometimes sneaky germs find a way into your body, through your mouth, nose, or ears, or even through a cut in your skin. That's when you need your defender cells!

Every day of your life, about one billion defender cells are made in the marrow in the center of your bones.

Can you believe that?

MY HEROES!!

THE DEFENDERS

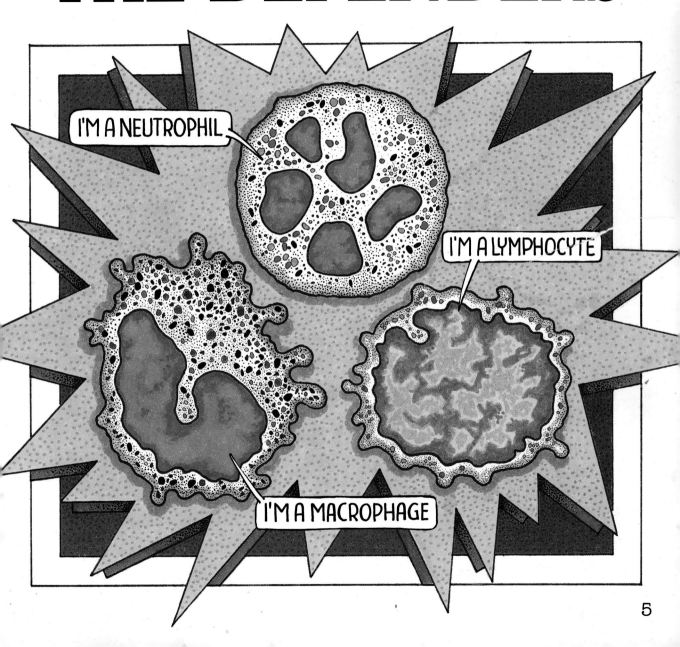

Neutrophils (NOO-tro-filz) are cells that are full of chemicals that destroy germs. They travel through the bloodstream, armed and ready to destroy germs that make you sick.

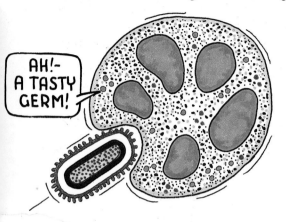

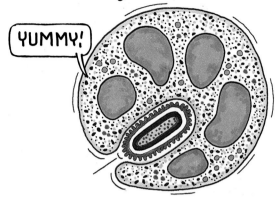

When a neutrophil detects an invading germ...

it gobbles it up and zaps it with deadly chemicals.

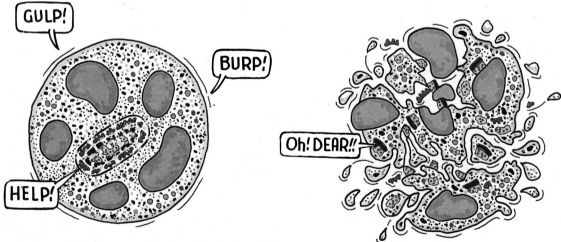

This destroys the germ, but unfortunately...

the neutrophil is sometimes destroyed too.

Don't worry, there are lots more where that one came from!

Macrophages (MAK-ruh-fay-jez) are like mobile garbage disposal units. They clean up whenever you are ill or injured, or wherever germs and dirt collect inside your body.

They travel around your bloodstream and then settle down in different parts of your body. There are millions in your lungs, for instance – eating up the dust and germs that you breathe in every day.

Like neutrophils, macrophages are full of germ-zapping chemicals, but they live a lot longer. Unlike neutrophils, they don't usually self-destruct.

Before they completely destroy the germ they have captured, macrophages may be helped by the other defender cells – the **lymphocytes** (LIM-fuh-sytz). Lymphocytes may join the battle if there's trouble afoot.

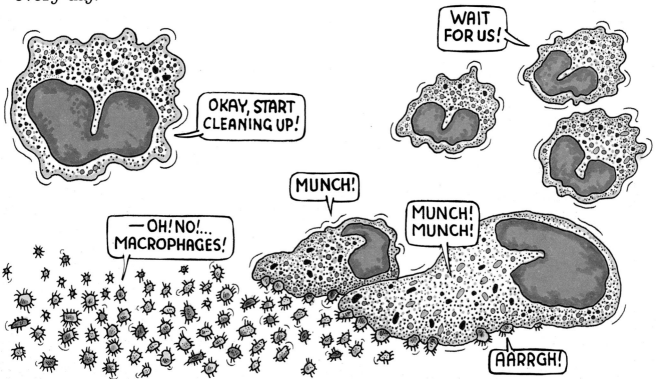

Lymphocytes are the smartest of all your defender cells. They don't all attack every germ they meet. Instead, there is a different group of lymphocytes for each different type of germ.

Every type of germ that invades your body carries its own identification marks, and you have a lymphocyte squad already programmed to fight each of these. Each group of lymphocytes recognizes the particular type of germ that it can attack.

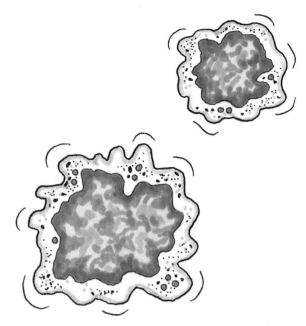

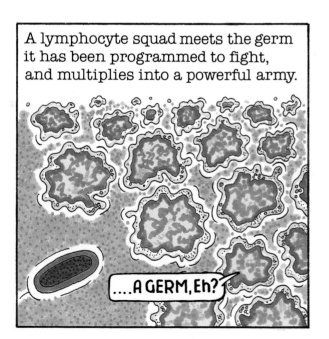

A lymphocyte squad meets the germ it has been programmed to fight, and multiplies into a powerful army.

....A GERM, Eh?

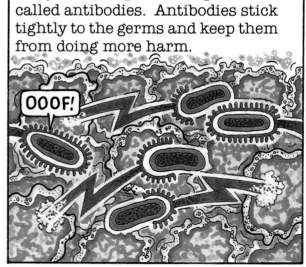

Some cells in the lymphocyte army release special weapons called antibodies. Antibodies stick tightly to the germs and keep them from doing more harm.

OOOF!

Other cells in the lymphocyte army turn into destroyers. Their task is to seek out and kill off cells that have been invaded by germs.

The struggle is over, and the lymphocyte squad is stronger than before. Some of these lymphocytes become memory lymphocytes and remain on alert deep inside the body for years.

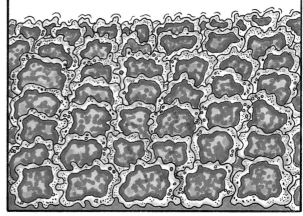

If the same germs try to invade again, the lymphocyte squad is ready for them. The battle is then won more easily. That's why most children have only one attack of chicken pox.

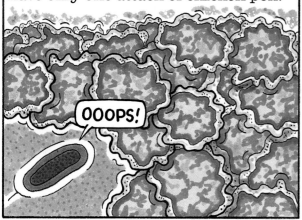

Neutrophils, macrophages, and lymphocytes must all fight side by side to win the cell wars.

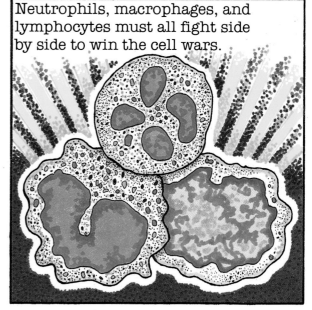

Viruses are public enemy number one. They invade your body and cause all sorts of diseases. They come in some weird and wonderful shapes.

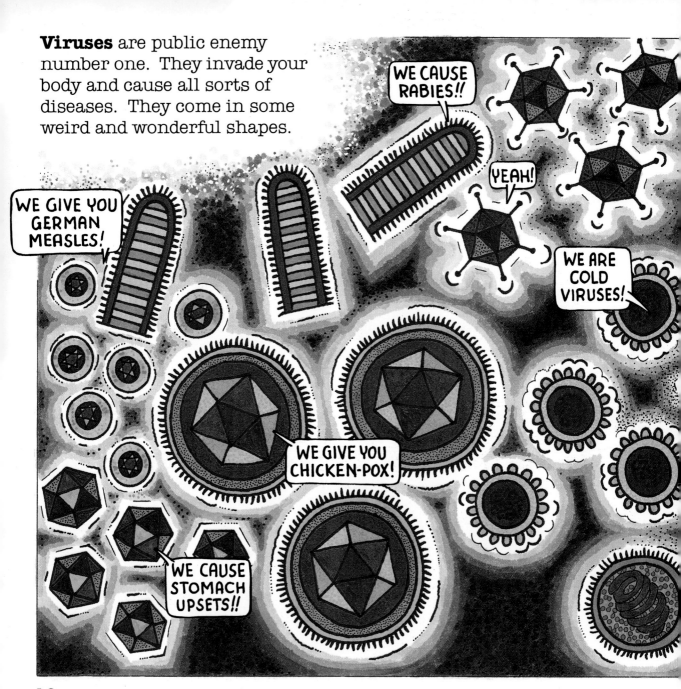

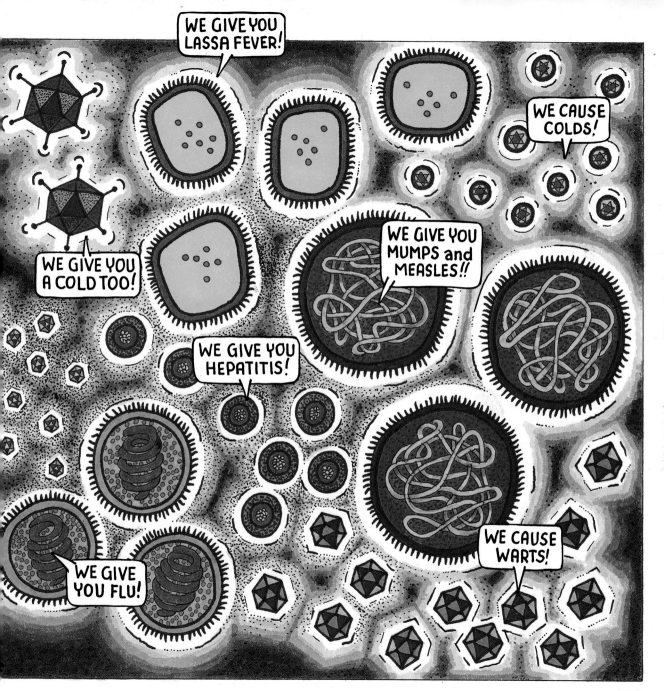

Viruses are germs that make you ill by entering your body, invading healthy cells, and turning them into virus-making cells.

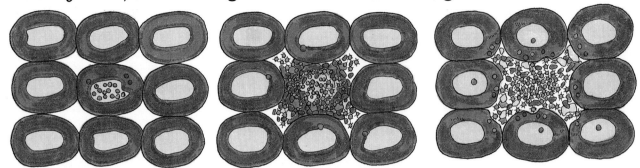

Then, instead of doing the jobs they're supposed to do, healthy cells start to produce viruses that invade more and more cells...

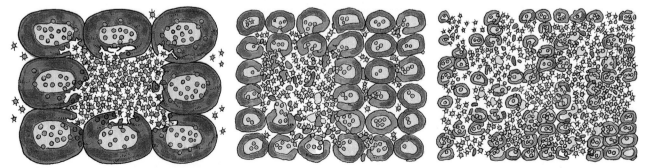

that make more and more viruses that invade more and more cells...

Viruses are very, very small, even smaller than the cells in your body. If one of your cells was this big (½ inch),

you'd be as tall as the Empire State Building, but if a cold virus was this big (½ inch), you'd be sneezing among the stars!

BLESS YOU!

13

WATCH OUT!!
Millions of cold viruses are
now on their way to invade and
destroy the cells of your nose
and breathing passages.

Let's look up your nose
and see what happens...

14

The cells inside your nose are always ready for trouble. They produce a gloppy fluid called mucus that traps viruses and other invaders. Mucus contains those special lymphocyte weapons, antibodies. Tiny, hairy parts of the nose cell surface waft the germs, antibodies, and mucus away.

But sometimes a few viruses sneak through the mucus and invade the cells inside your nose. They turn the nose cells into virus-makers. Different viruses then attack more cells. Some nose cells die. Others produce watery stuff that makes you sneeze and feel all stuffed up.

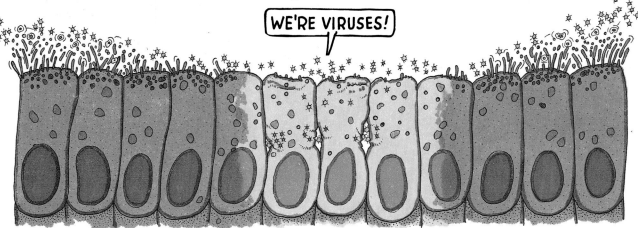

Don't worry! Those viruses are soon spotted by your defender cells. They rush into your nose and try to destroy as many viruses as they can.

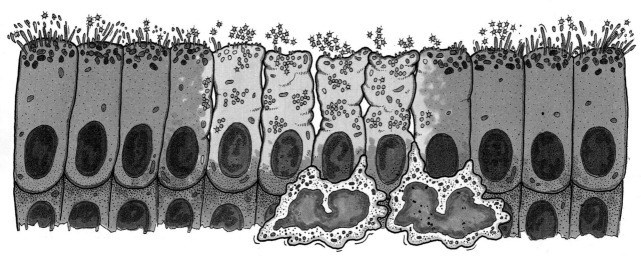

Macrophages and neutrophils, as well as your nose cells, send out chemical signals. These signals protect nearby cells from the cold virus and call lymphocytes to the trouble zone.

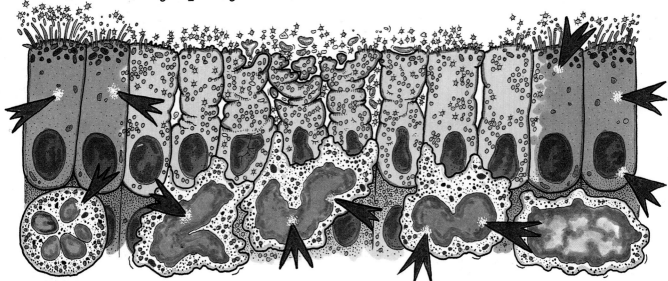

Now on full alert, the cold virus squad of your lymphocytes is rapidly multiplying. Soon you have thousands and thousands of lymphocytes programmed to destroy cells that have been invaded by viruses.

Lymphocytes release antibodies that coat the cold virus. Once a cold virus is coated with its antibody, it can't invade any more cells, and it gets gobbled up quickly by neutrophils and macrophages.

So it's not surprising that colds and other virus infections go away, since you've got all those hard-working defender cells inside you.

   But your defender cells have other enemies – **bacteria!**

Bacteria are public enemy number two! They are smaller than human cells but much bigger than viruses. Bacteria are found everywhere – in the air, in the ocean, in rivers, in the soil, on your skin, on your teeth, even inside you! Most of these bacteria are not your enemies. In fact, they are an important part of nature. Some helpful bacteria that live in your body help you to digest the food you eat.

But some types of bacteria are very harmful. If they get inside your body, they multiply quickly and release poisons that can make you very sick.

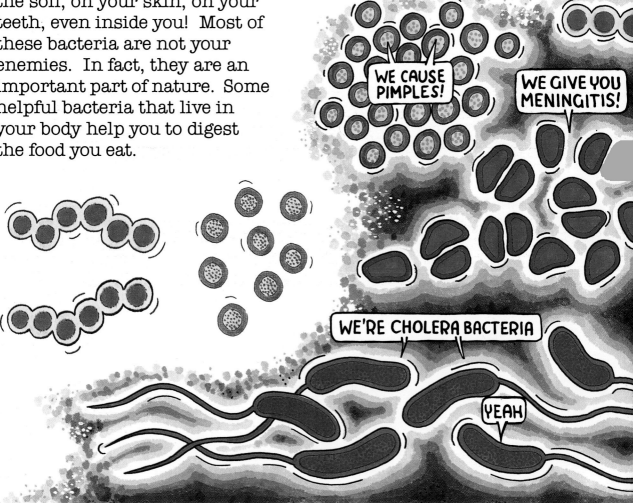

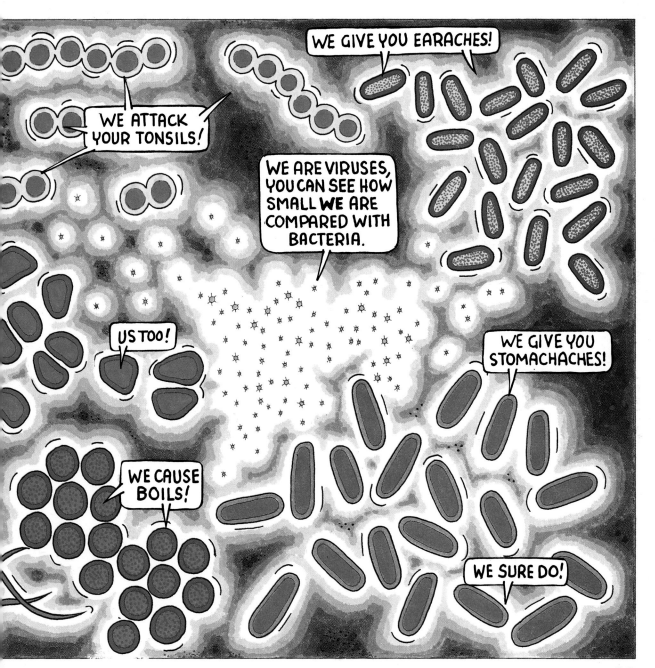

19

One way that harmful bacteria can get into your body is in food that has not been stored or cooked properly. Imagine this... You put a raw chicken and some ham in the refrigerator. Dangerous bacteria live inside the chicken, but the cold air in the fridge keeps them from multiplying. The chicken is dripping onto the ham. The ham now has some bacteria on it – but not enough to hurt you. That would take at least a million.

Then you make some ham sandwiches for your school lunch the next day. You leave them on the table. Overnight, the bacteria start to multiply.

After twenty minutes, each bacterium has become two. After another twenty minutes, two become four. By the morning there are over two million sneaky bacteria in your ham sandwiches! You enjoy your sandwiches at lunch. But little do you know what else is inside them! During the afternoon, the bacteria keep multiplying inside you. They stick to the cells that line your stomach and make poisons that destroy cells.

In the middle of the night, you feel really sick. Don't panic! Your defender cells fight back. Neutrophils and macrophages find bacteria just as tasty as viruses.

And lymphocytes love a good fight with bacteria.

Although you feel groggy, your defender cells are still fighting the bacteria and their poisons. With some rest and plenty to drink, you soon feel much better.

SO REMEMBER:
Keep food covered in the refrigerator. Raw foods may contain dangerous bacteria, but these are killed by thorough cooking. Wash your hands, kitchen tools, and kitchen surfaces after handling raw food.

Scientists and doctors have found a very smart way of protecting you from viruses and bacteria, with help from your defender cells. It's called **vaccination** (vak-sih-NAY-shun). They have created harmless germs in the laboratory. These germs look just like the real germs that the doctors want to protect you from.

When the harmless germs are given to young children, a lymphocyte squad is quickly alerted. This squad multiplies into a strong army that attacks the harmless germ. Then if the real germs ever attack you after you have been vaccinated, you already have an army of lymphocytes ready to protect you. Unfortunately, scientists haven't been able to find vaccines (vak-SEENZ) for all troublesome germs. The sneaky flu virus, for example, keeps changing its identification marks. And there are over a hundred different viruses that cause colds!

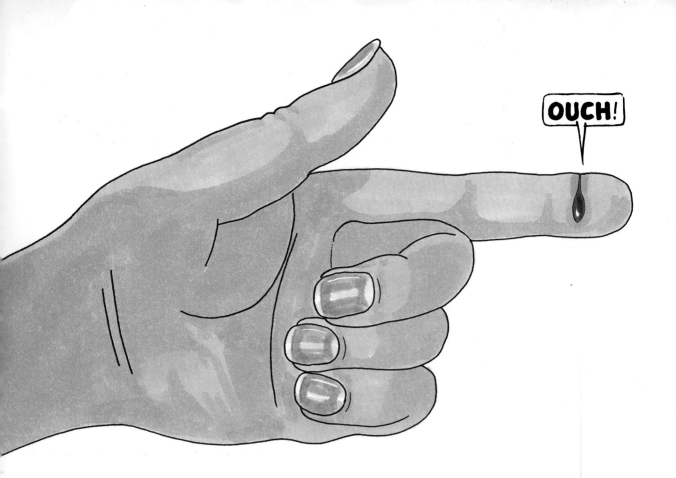

Defender cells don't just work together to fight illnesses. They also help repair your body if it gets damaged.

Imagine you've just cut your finger. It bleeds because you have cut through some of the tiny tubes (called capillaries) that carry blood among your skin cells. The blood soon becomes dark and sticky. It stops flowing and forms a blood clot. The blood clot dries and shrinks, pulling the edges of the cut together – that's what a scab is.

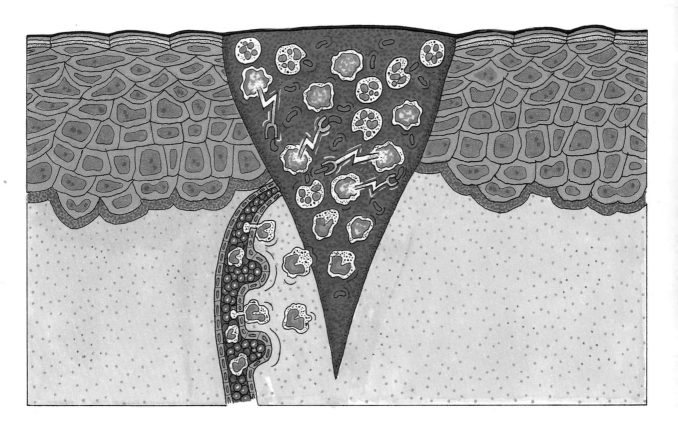

If harmful bacteria and viruses get into the cut, they have to be zapped! Chemical messages released by injured cells alert neutrophils and lymphocytes. They leave the bloodstream by the thousands and move into the clot, hunting for germs.

After twenty-four hours, the macrophages start to move in. They get to work, cleaning up dead cells, live bacteria, and clotted blood. Blood vessel cells begin to divide and make a new blood supply for the cut.

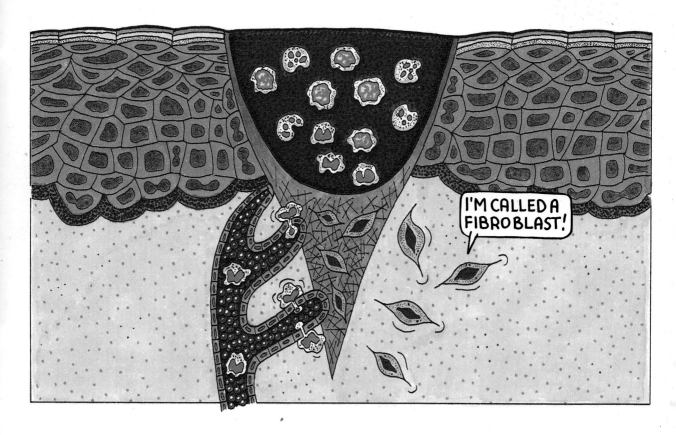

After about three days, your defender cells have cleaned up the cut very well, and all danger of infection is past. It is then that the skin's builder cells — **fibroblasts** — are brought into action. Fibroblasts are long, thin cells. They make special strengthening strands that pull the broken skin together.

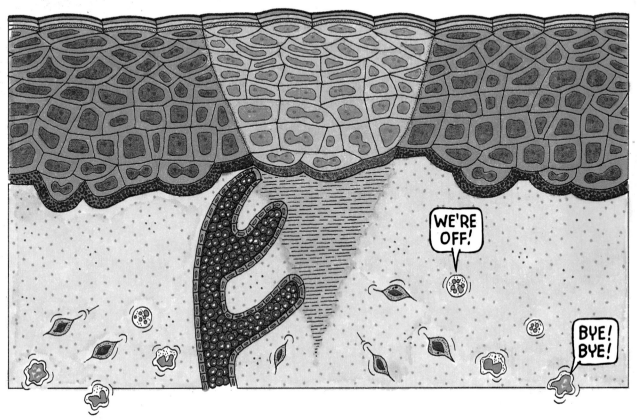

Slowly the defender cells and fibroblasts disappear. They have done their job. Now the new skin cells take over, growing out from the edge of the cut.

Sometimes, however, a wound might be deep, and then your cells can't cope so well. In that case, a doctor can help by putting in stitches.

This isn't the whole story of your defender cells. They also fight bigger enemies, like funguses and tapeworms. They help broken bones to mend, they eat up dead and dying cells, and they even get rid of pimples. Now you don't have to worry about germs that try to make you sick! You know your defender cells are always ready to fight **CELL WARS!!**

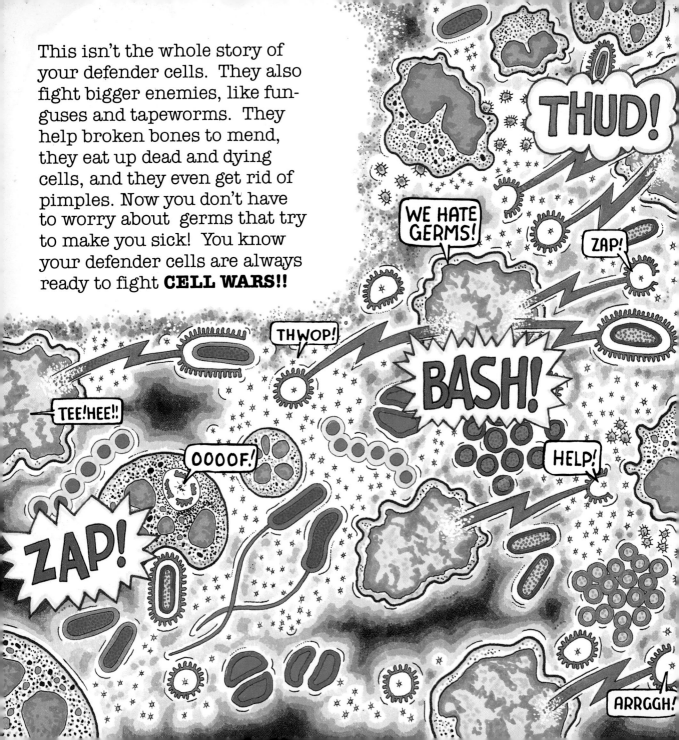